MW00638414

Hope looks good on you!

A Comedian's Joy-inducing Daily Devotional for Women

. . . . .

DORIE MCLEMORE

Red Bird Press

Published by Red Bird Press
www.redbirdpress.org

THE HOLY BIBLE, NEW
INTERNATIONAL VERSION®, NIV®
Copyright © 1973, 1978, 1984, 2011 by
Biblica, Inc.™ Used by permission. All
rights reserved worldwide.

Scripture quotations marked NLT are taken
from the Holy Bible, New Living
Translation, copyright © 1996, 2004, 2015
by Tyndale House Foundation. Used by
permission of Tyndale House Publishers,
Inc., Carol Stream, Illinois 60188. All rights
reserved.

Scripture quotations marked MSG are
taken from THE MESSAGE, copyright ©
1993, 2002, 2018 by Eugene H. Peterson.
Used by permission of NavPress. All rights
reserved. Represented by Tyndale House
Publishers, Inc.

ISBN: 978-1-7362194-1-6

Dedication

This book is dedicated to all my family and friends
who either endured living through a "Dorie story" or
hearing it told over and over!
Also to anyone who could use some hope right now.
There's always hope!

Contents

vi

1: Names

I'm not good with names. To be accurate, I'm not good with faces either. Some people say, "I'm not good with names, but I never forget a face."

Not so with me.

I could see my child's teacher in a dentist office and not recognize her because she is outside the school property!

This fact can lead to some pretty embarrassing moments. One such incident occurred when my husband and I were working as youth pastors in the city of Boston.

We had taken our youth group to a convention where other church groups would

1

come from all over the East coast.

At the end of a session, I saw her walking towards me. I couldn't believe it — I had not seen Sarah in years!

Sarah and I had gone on my very first mission trip together, spending weeks in Brazil when we were sixteen. For years, we called, wrote, and visited. I didn't expect to see her here, but what a great surprise!

I ran up to her, screaming.
I hugged her — hard.

I pulled her away, looked at her face, and screamed again. Then, I involved her in some sort of happy dance that evoked the attention of the crowd around us.

I knew we looked silly, but I didn't care — it was Sarah!

At this point, my husband joined the crowd and interrupted our dance of joy to ask, "Dorie, what is going on?"

I answered, almost crying, "Bryan...this is my friend, *Sarah*, from my trip to Brazil!"

Then, I heard it.
"No, I'm not."

Suddenly, all became clear. I recognized her and remembered who she was — someone I had met once or twice in college. It would have been easier if I had not known her at all!

I awkwardly released her from the dance position and tried making regular conversation. I have no recollection of what was said. Thankfully, the crowd around us eventually dispersed.

Names are important. I'm grateful that God doesn't have my struggle remembering our names...or faces!

In fact, it says in the book of Isaiah that God has written our names on the palm of His hand. I don't think it was to help Him remember them, though! I like to picture Him lovingly doodling our names there.

Isaiah was a prophet to the Jewish people and wrote these words during their exile to Babylon. They were forced out of their homeland and were living in a foreign land for seventy years.

I had the privilege of sharing this message with a group of refugee women in Cyprus. They could relate to the Israelites being forced to leave their home countries and live in an unknown land. They felt forgotten by God. But Isaiah had a message for them...

"The Lord has deserted us; the Lord has forgotten us."
"Never! Can a mother forget her nursing child? Can she feel no love for the child she has borne? But even if that were possible, I would not forget you! See, I have written your name on the palms of my hands."
Isaiah 49:14-16 NLT

We may not be exiled to a foreign land, but we can sometimes find ourselves in a foreign place in our lives, maybe a new season.

I recently entered one of those new seasons. Our son had turned eighteen and enlisted in the army reserves...this is definitely a foreign place for this mama! Wasn't he just playing with plastic army men on his bedroom floor a minute ago?

It's in these foreign places, these new seasons, that God reminds us that He has not forgotten us.

Reflect & journal:

Are you in a foreign place right now, facing a new season of life? Take a moment to write out a time when you might have felt that way. Then, remember that you have hope knowing that God has not forgotten you — He has written your name on His hands!

Draw a picture of a hand and write your name on it for a good visual to help you remember that truth today!

. . .

2: Dollhouse Reno

I don't consider myself to be a DIY-er. I don't tend to make pretty things with my hands. I will, however, attempt it when it will save money.

This was the case when I had it in my head to get my girls a dollhouse one Christmas.

I had never been in the market for a dollhouse before and had a case of severe sticker shock.

New construction was pricey and the kits to build from the ground up were daunting. So, I decided to look at some pre-owned homes.

I didn't realize that I would be buying a fixer upper.

I found the pre-owned model on one of those websites with a classified section and drove out to see it. It had good bones so I decided to make the investment even though I could see it was going to need some TLC and a good amount of elbow grease.

Getting started, I had wanted an open floor plan, but I couldn't tell if the walls were load-bearing so I left the structure the same.

Yep, I am still talking about a dollhouse.

I was really hoping there were hardwood floors under that hot pink felt. There had been cat hair so that flooring had to go.

After a strenuous demo day removing the hot glue, there they were — hardwood floors! They had really taken a beating from the previous owners so I wanted to find out how to bring back their original luster.

So, I embarked on a trip to Home Depot® to talk to their flooring experts.

I was talking to one of their associates in the flooring department and he suggested I use a wax product to bring back the shine. He pointed to a vat of it.

Trying to hide the actual size of my project, I asked if it came in something...smaller.

He told me it also came in a quart-size, but that I would need several quarts to cover any floorspace.

Again, I asked if the product came in something...smaller.

This is when he asked me how many square feet I was trying to cover.

My answer: "two; or maybe one and a half."

This is when he found out I was working on a dollhouse renovation.

Then, he stopped talking to me.

Sometimes I feel like a real project...like God must think I'm a fixer upper.

It's as if He looked at me and thought, "I'm going to need a nap after this one." I like that God took a nap after creation, but that's besides the point.

The truth is that God didn't try to fix us up. He made us new.

"This means that anyone who belongs to Christ has become a new person. The old life is gone; a new life has begun! And all of this is a gift from God, who brought us back to Himself through Christ. And God has given us this task of reconciling people to Him."
2 Corinthians 5:17-18 NLT

He gave us a gift of a new life in Him after reconciling us back to Himself!   We might think we are a piece of work or just too much of a project, but God has already made us new.

I think we get wrapped up in our own issues at times and forget that not only has God given us this gift, but that He has also given us a task to offer it to others who might need some TLC and could use the power of God to make them new.

My husband and I do some house-flipping...the non-dollhouse kind.   We see homes in shambles and we can see where the owners had made failed attempts to fix things and where they had lost hope.

I can imagine there are people walking around feeling that way inside...that there are just too many broken things and hope is lost.

We need to share the good news with them

that there is an "investor" who sees something brand new. They just need to give Him the keys!

Reflect & journal:

Have you ever felt like you were a "project" to God? Is there an area of your life that you still need to hand over the keys? Take a few moments to write out your thoughts about these questions.

. . .

3: Friendship Bread

I decided to start a friendship bread dough nursery. Actually, nobody decides that...it was thrust upon me.

Have you ever heard of "Amish friendship bread?" Me neither. That is until my mother-in-law gave me the beginnings of what would become my dough hatchery.

Friendship bread is an Amish sweet bread recipe-turned-chain-letter. It is a TEN-day recipe. The idea is that someone makes the bread starter that gets passed out to unsuspecting people...I mean, friends.

Then, for nine days, the recipe calls for kneading and feeding the starter more ingredients in order to produce more starter for more friends.

On the tenth day, the dough can be split into four gallon-size bags and given out to others who will then continue the pattern in this never-ending cycle of bread and friendship.

This is all well and good if you have friends who enjoy ten-day recipes.

I have non-committal friends, late friends, and friends who like to procrastinate.

So, I waited...and continued to watch and feed and knead and babysit my four friends' friendship bread dough starters. Then, day number ten came again ... four gallon bags of starter turned into *sixteen*!

My kitchen counter housed my dough daycare. I couldn't abandon it now — I was too invested. Each day I would feed my sixteen foster bags and make calls to find homes.

But it was *coming* — day number ten was again on the horizon! I knew I couldn't keep this up. I was about to have *sixty-four* bags of friendship bread dough!

I started to wonder if I could make this into a business — selling Amish bread from my non-Amish apartment?

What to do? I couldn't just let this friendship dough die and then forever be labeled as the end of the friendship chain! Yes, I would be the one that killed the yeast used for generations of bread and friends.

So, on day eight, I made the notes that I attached to the bags that I left on the doorsteps.

"To a good home," they read. Don't worry, I was sure to include the ten-day recipe.

Then, I went on my secret mission, delivering my dough babies to sixteen lucky neighbors.

Later a "friend" asked why I didn't just make the dough into bread and stop the cycle.

Wait — that was an option?!

Expectations. How many times have expectations got us into a mess...not just the dough kind.

So many expectations.

Expectations from family, friends, society, expectations we place on ourselves. Expectations that we believe God has put on our lives.

It can be overwhelming. We can run into the trap of guilt and shame and failure when we feel as though we are falling short of these expectations.

The truth is that God cannot love us more or less than He does right now. His love is not based on performance.

Our status as His children doesn't change if we don't volunteer at every church event or if we don't feel like we measure up as parents, as spouses, as friends.

We don't need to earn the love He already freely gives us.

I love how the psalmist writes these beautiful lyrics about God's faithful love:

"I will sing of the Lord's unfailing love forever! Young and old will hear of your faithfulness. Your unfailing love will last forever. Your faithfulness is as enduring as the heavens."
Psalms 89:1-2 NLT

(Note: the actual Amish Friendship bread recipe I used is available in the back of the book so you, too, can start your own dough daycare.)

Reflect & journal:

How do the expectations of others influence you? Take a moment now to write these expectations down. Then, in large print across all of them, write the words: I AM LOVED.

. . .

4: High School Robbery

Maybe don't wear a ski mask near a bank — it's just a bad idea. It wouldn't have otherwise crossed my mind to wear a ski mask near a bank, but I was in the newspaper class my senior year in high school and was sometimes overzealous.

I loved my role as the photographer because it meant I had a press pass that I could use to get out of classes so I could photograph all the campus happenings and hang out in the dark room.

Yes, we used real film in the dark ages of the 1990s.

As a school newspaper staff, we rarely got to

cover any hot topics or do any investigative reporting. This piece of journalism revolved around science fair findings, football scoreboards, and the occasional cafeteria food review.

So, we jumped at the chance to cover a story about a local bank robbery.

My fellow photographer friend and I planned our excursion to take pictures of the bank. I'm not sure if we were more excited that we would be leaving school in the middle of classes or because this story could be our big break.

We got too excited.
We weren't thinking clearly.
When one of us suggested we dress up as the bank robber, the other of us didn't stop it.
We packed a costume.

If you ever pack a costume to go to a bank, something has gone awry.

Somewhere during the process, I volunteered to wear the all-black outfit and knit ski mask. *This will be fun*, I thought.

My friend decided that it might be a good

idea to tell the bank people what we wanted to do before I came in wearing my robber costume.

This was the only good idea we had that day.

The bank people had one good idea and then one not-so-great idea. They told her we couldn't come inside to take the robber pictures in case their security cameras picked it up, but we could take the photos right outside the bank.

We started the posing.

We involved a prop: a big bag with a money sign drawn on the outside of it.

I acted it out, running from the bank in slow motion with my bag-o-money in hand.

After the photo shoot was over, we decided to reward ourselves by going across the street to the gas station store to get some ice cream. We recapped our brilliant plan and reveled in our triumph in journalism.

It was then that I heard the tapping. Tap-tap on the car door window. Then something that sounded like, "Step out of the vehicle."

My friend and I froze with our ice cream still in-hand, my black ski mask perched on the top of my head so my face could lick said ice cream.

We opened the car doors and saw the sheriff standing there, reading us our Miranda rights, handcuffs at the ready. "You have the right to remain silent..."

Silent, we weren't.

We broke out into a panicked frenzy as we tried to tell him our story. We did our best to convince him that we were reporters from the school paper, and not the hardened criminals that he supposed us to be.

It didn't take a lot of convincing.

He took one look at our home-made robber costume and the bag-o-money lying on the seat of our car and possibly took into consideration that we were holding ice cream cones, and deducted that we were probably not criminal masterminds.

He put down his handcuffs and then told us that someone had seen us in front of the bank and called in a robbery. He did not look happy when he added, "...And now I have to go call off the brigade of state troopers who are already on their way."

He informed us that the SWAT team would have arrived next.

Lessons were learned that day:

#1 There are very few acceptable times to wear a ski mask in public.

#2 If you are interrogated by a police officer, it helps to be holding ice cream.

#3 If you do ever rob a bank, don't get the ice cream across the street from the bank.

#4 Probably don't actually rob a bank.

We did end up with a great story in the school newspaper which had more to do with the near-arrest of a few students than the actual bank robbery.

Luckily, bank robbery is not a typical issue most people struggle with on a normal basis. Unfortunately, though, we do tend to allow ourselves to be *robbed* of joy, peace, and hope in our lives.

Jesus describes this kind of robbery in John chapter ten that takes place in a pasture crime scene, complete with sheep and rolling hills. He loved using illustrations that His audience would understand as many families in Bible times would have owned herds of animals.

He describes how thieves come in to the sheepfold by sneaking over the wall instead of coming in through the gate like the shepherd.

I think we allow robbers to sneak in over the walls of our hearts. We let worry, fear, and anxiety sneak in. We let anger and doubt sneak in. We let comparison and jealousy sneak in over the walls.

We can be tricked into listening to their voices rather than the voice of the true shepherd.

Jesus is the Good Shepherd in the story, He comes in through the gate. The gatekeeper opens the gate wide for him and the sheep know his voice. He explains that He is more than just a hired hand, He cares for his sheep and would sacrifice His life for them.

Jesus reveals the true purpose of these robbers and the heart of the Good Shepherd in verse ten:

*"The thief's purpose is to steal and kill and destroy.
My purpose is to give them a rich and satisfying life."
John 10:10 NLT*

God is so good. He knows that when we
follow His voice as our Good Shepherd, we
will have an abundant life.

Let's stop allowing robbers to sneak in over
the walls or listen to the voices of fear, worry,
doubt, anger, and others who just want to
steal from our lives!

Reflect & journal:

Take time to reflect and answer the question: what "robbers" are you allowing to sneak in over your heart walls? And how can you begin listening more for the voice of God, your Good Shepherd?

(Note: the robbers will probably not be wearing actual black knit ski masks)

. . .

5: Ski Patrol

You don't need skiing lessons. Those are words that should not be placed consecutively in the same sentence. But alas, my newlywed husband uttered them confidently to his new bride.

After being thrust onto a pile of lumber tied into a pulley system that they call a "ski lift," I dangled high above the snow drifts and trees below.

As I reached the mountainous peak, I survived getting off the ski lift without being struck by the next passengers...which is a feat by itself.

The momentum I had gained getting off of

the lift transferred into forward motion, leading to my immediate descent down the slope.

I began to pick up speed as I got into the only ski position I had seen on the Winter Olympics: knees bent, ski poles pointed backwards, head down.

I was going quite fast and started to believe that I might be a natural or some sort of speed-skier prodigy.

It was also at this point in time that I realized I didn't know how to slow down...or steer. I began flailing my arms and yelling to warn upcoming skiers.

Men, women, and children in my path were diving to safety.

At that moment, I recalled the only instruction my husband had felt was important to note: how to stop. I seemed to remember him saying something about the skis...like I was supposed to cross them.

It didn't make sense from an engineering perspective, but from an I-need-to-stop-before-I-fall-off-a-cliff perspective, I was willing to try it.

So I did it.
I crossed my skis.

My husband told me later that it looked like: head, legs, head, legs, head, legs...then a yard sale of various ski equipment strewn down the slope.

I knocked myself out and came to with my husband standing over me asking, "Are you ready to try again?"

My response: "get ski patrol."

I was carted off that bunny slope in a toboggan sled.

So, maybe I needed a bit of instruction — from an actual instructor. In life, sometimes we can feel a bit in over our heads, flailing down a slope at breakneck speed. This is when we might look ahead and start to worry.

I like how it says in the book of Matthew that we shouldn't worry about tomorrow because we have enough worries for today.

"So don't worry about tomorrow, for tomorrow will

bring its own worries. Today's trouble is enough for
today."
Matthew 6:34 NLT

He knew we are not in 'tomorrow' yet...only God is in tomorrow.   It's comforting to think that God already has been to tomorrow — we aren't headed there alone or to somewhere He hasn't already been.

One of my favorite quotes is by Corrie Ten Boom, the Holocaust survivor whose family helped many Jews escape the Nazis by hiding them in their home.

Her book, <u>The Hiding Place</u>, tells her story and how she was able to find hope in God even after her family was betrayed and was imprisoned in a concentration camp during the Holocaust.[1]

She later shared some of her thoughts and beliefs in a devotional book called, <u>Clippings from My Notebook</u>, where she shares this powerful insight about worry:

"Worry does not empty tomorrow of its sorrow; it empties today of its strength."[2]
— Corrie Ten Boom

If Corrie Ten Boom can live through the horrors of the Holocaust and pen those words, it makes them all that much more compelling.

Worry is not productive. It produces nothing and it can't be saved up and redeemed for courage later. I heard it also said that worrying about a circumstance is like living through the difficult experience twice.

We cannot worry ahead of a situation and expect to make progress.

We need to take one day at a time...one bunny slope after one bunny slope. Also, spend time listening to our Instructor — God might know a thing or two about these slopes that we need to maneuver through!

And...possibly learn how to stop.
(Stop worrying, that is!)

Reflect & journal:

What worries make you feel like you are careening down the hill with no control? Take a few minutes to make a list and ask for the Instructor's help in navigating through them without the worry.

. . .

6: The Dollar Store

So, I'm at the dollar store...the *real* dollar store where every item is actually one dollar. I'm a frugal person and this is my paradise. I walk around like I own the place.

I throw items into my cart with such confidence knowing that I can buy anything in this store — and I do.

I could bankrupt my family at the Dollar Tree®.

Not so much at Macy's® or Nordstrom® because I won't even go into stores like those. They are just my gateway to the mall. I almost run through them so I don't accidentally break something and have to pay for it!

But not so with the Dollar Tree®.

I always stay in the dollar store too long. I seem to think it's some kind of requirement to go up and down every aisle. Sometimes I'm in there so long, I know the store employees are thinking, 'she is definitely stealing stuff.'

Although I have never actually stolen anything from a dollar store, some of the deals feel like a steal! Portable soap dishes, 'silk' flowers, potpourri, discontinued make-up, 1000 staples and mini stapler sets, rain ponchos, multi-colored chip clips...for a dollar?

How are they making any money on this stuff?

Okay, I admit that I haven't bought potpourri in years. I'm not sure why they are still selling it.

My favorite, though, is the as-seen-on-tv section. I love infomercials, but I wait to buy the products at the dollar store...because that's when you know they *really work*.

It was there in the middle of one of my lengthy dollar store shopping trips that I felt God speak to my heart and whisper something like:

'Why do you walk with confidence through the dollar-store-level issues in your life, but when it comes to the Macy's-level issues, you still walk in so much fear? Don't you know I am big enough, my shoulders are wide enough, and even your biggest problems look small to Me?'

Only God would know to speak to me with a shopping metaphor!

It was the truth. I had been able to trust Him with the small stuff...the things I could almost handle on my own.

I had easily navigated through minor illnesses, everyday bills, and the ups and downs of my teenagers' emotions, but I found myself struggling with anxiety when it came to the *big stuff* and the uncertainty of the future as if God doesn't have what it takes for those types of things.

In this season, my son had turned seventeen and my father had turned seventy and I realized that neither would be young forever. I was exiting one stage of life that I felt like I had just figured out; and I was entering a new stage of life that I didn't feel ready for.

I was waking up morning after morning with anxiety and fear to the point that my chest would hurt and feel like there was an actual weight on it.

Maybe since I hadn't been spending much time in prayer those mornings, God had to meet me in the dollar store!

He was trying to show me that I didn't need to walk around in fear — that no issue was too big for Him, no burden was too heavy, no part of my future was unstable. I could walk freely through even the hard things of life with confidence knowing that truth.

I also read a verse in Proverbs 31 that became my motto during this struggle. I generally avoid this chapter in the Bible because the Proverbs 31 woman makes me look bad and I don't agree with some of her philosophies...like rising early!

But then I came across verse 25; truthfully, it was on a mug that a friend gave me or I would have never seen it:

*"She is clothed with strength and dignity, and she
laughs without fear of the future."*
Proverbs 31:25 NLT

How could she laugh without fear of the
future? It's not as if Old Testament days were
care-free back then or that there wasn't plenty
she could worry about. They didn't even
have ibuprofen. Her future could be bleak.

Maybe God met her in the dollar store, too.

She hadn't even read the verse in Romans
8:38 yet, but God must have known we would
struggle with fears and worries because Paul
includes fears for today and worries about
tomorrow in the list of things that can't
separate us from God's love:

*"And I am convinced that nothing can ever separate us
from God's love. Neither death nor life, neither angels
nor demons, neither our fears for today nor our worries
about tomorrow—not even the powers of hell can
separate us from God's love."*
Romans 8:38 NLT

I don't know how I missed that all these years.
I had even learned a song and memorized
that verse, but never noticed the part about
fears and worries.

God is so faithful. He uses dollar store trips and mugs and Bible verse songs to teach us truths about His character and who He is.

I think that the reason that the Proverbs 31 woman was able to laugh without fear of the future was because she *knew God*.

She knew His character.
She knew He is love.
She knew He cares for her.
She knew He is big enough.
She knew He held her future.

The more we know Him, the more we will trust Him and the more we will walk with confidence through anything our future holds.

> *"Cast all your anxiety on Him because*
> *He cares for you."*
> *1 Peter 5:7 NIV*

Maybe I will go back to the dollar store to see if God wants to chat some more...and I'm out of potpourri.

Reflect & journal:

What "big stuff" can you start trusting God with? Take a few moments to list them out and then write over them: "Laugh without fear!"

. . .

7: Six-hour Side Dish

Honey, *why don't I just make the pasta salad for the luncheon?* Did I actually just say that out loud? There were plenty of reasons I shouldn't offer to make any real food for a group of sixty people.

It was too late...my husband was impressed.

Looking at the recipe card, it didn't seem like a major project. Until, of course, I *quintupled* it.

I often do this to myself — use a recipe I've never even attempted and then multiply the ingredients using some form of algebra I haven't done in twenty years.

Each time I do something like that, I vow to never do it to myself again which lasts just long enough until I forget what it was like the first time...sort of like childbirth.

So, it started.

Converting one box of pasta noodles to five boxes, turns the manageable five hard-boiled eggs into twenty-five, the six stalks of celery into thirty, and so on down the ingredient list.

I also have this habit of severely underestimating the amount of time a project will take so I didn't boil my first egg until ten o'clock at night.

I figured, 'how long could it possibly take? It's a side dish.'

About three hours into the ordeal, I realized that I couldn't fit the pasta that I had boiled in shifts into any one bowl that I owned.

I also realized that I couldn't construct the math on the rest of the ingredients if I split the noodles into several different containers, so I looked for something large enough to house my growing culinary nightmare.

It was late and I already wanted to quit. I desperately wanted to go to bed and join my husband in his slumber, but once you *start* making pasta salad for sixty people, how do you *stop*?!

With newfound determination, I spotted a storage tub that was being used for organizational purposes, emptied out the office supplies and thrust it into the world of kitchenware.

I spilled all the noodles from the different pots into this enormous container and got back to shelling my twenty-five hard-boiled eggs.

TWO WHOLE HOURS later, I realized as I poured the wet ingredients over the pasta that I did not have an utensil long enough to stir it! The longest spoon I had in my drawers did not reach the bottom of the tub and felt more like an oar as I rowed it through my sea of noodles.

I had come too far to let this stop me.

So, I rolled up my sleeves, washed my arms, and combined it by hand — *literally*.

I began to laugh at the sight of myself sitting

on the floor next to my tub of pasta salad; celery and hard-boiled egg pieces still clinging to my forearms. That is, until a certain question came into my head: "How am I going to refrigerate this?"

This type of question does not occur to me soon enough in most cases.

It was close to four o'clock in the morning — late enough for me to be delirious, but not late enough for the pasta salad to make it unrefrigerated until my husband could get it to the church's commercial kitchen.

In a moment of desperation, I found myself throwing bags of frozen peas and carrots and corn on top of the tub that housed the pasta salad.

Then, exhausted by the noodle all-nighter, I collapsed in bed.

How confused my husband must have been when he walked into the kitchen that next morning to see our storage tub filled with pasta salad and covered by a mountain of frozen vegetables!

I'm not sure what happened, but somewhere

between looking at the recipe card and running the soggy noodles through my fingers, I had gotten in over my head.

It's in these kinds of circumstances that often the Scripture found in Proverbs comes to mind,

"Trust in the LORD with all your heart, And lean not on your own understanding; In all your ways acknowledge Him, And He shall direct your paths."
Proverbs 3:5-6 NKJV

So many times we try to do things on our own when God is just waiting in the wings to be acknowledged so we can follow His lead.

I could have acknowledged my weakness in the area of culinary arts and called my mother-in-law who would have given me the insight I needed to realize that people do not eat pasta salad by the quart.

She could have reminded me of the need for refrigeration before the four A.M. crisis.

I guess my resulting chaos is what happens when we lean on our own understanding...when we think we can handle it all without the help of Someone who knows more than us until we are sitting next to our soggy mess wondering what to do next.

It's better not to wait until you are elbow deep in a situation before acknowledging the One who knows all and holds the future in His hands.

His way is always best and doesn't usually involve impressing your husband — with a six-hour side dish.

Reflect & journal:

Are there soggy messes in your life that you need to surrender to God's wisdom?   Take a moment to write them down and allow Him to direct those paths.

. . .

8: Frames

So, it happened again. I blew it. Bad. My mommy skills were at an all-time low as I walked away from yelling at my son.

He probably did something that deserved correction, but not like that. I cried out to God in my normal fashion, something like: "God, have mercy!" (or as my youngest would repeat: "God, have *murphy*!")

This time seemed different — desperate. I didn't know how to get to a place where I could figure out what was happening.

Why the blow-ups? Why couldn't I get things under control? I had been a Christian for over thirty years...when does peace and patience kick in?

I would wrack my brain for the right Scriptures — was it the fruit of the Spirit, the Sermon on the Mount, the Lord's Prayer, the Last Supper? Why was this so hard?

I felt like in that moment, the Lord said, 'why don't you just start seeing your children and husband the way I see them?'

Sometimes God talks to me in pictures...He must know I'm a visual learner! I could see a mental image of a golden picture frame with nothing in it.

It was a beautiful and ornate frame on the outside, but the back of it was old and all the wall-hanging parts were exposed.

I felt like the Lord showed me that He saw my kids and husband through the ornate side of the frame, but it was as if I was looking at them with the frame turned around.

He had a whole different perspective of who they are. I realized in that moment that I had been believing lies over each of them and those lies were coloring the way I responded to them. I wasn't seeing their true identity and worth; instead, I only saw all their flaws.

I asked God to show me how He sees each of them. It was as if He whispered a word over them, and for some reason, they all started with the letter P...probably because God knows I need a way to remember things easier!

My son's word: "passionate." The problem was that I was seeing him as being argumentative, emotional, and angry, but God was revealing to me that He saw him as passionate.

When I turned the frame around and saw my son in this new light, I realized that he usually is only angry because he is passionate about something — and chores or other responsibilities are getting in the way of doing what he wants to do!

It doesn't excuse bad attitudes, but this new perspective helped me stop looking at just his faults and to start seeing his potential — being passionate can be a good thing!

My oldest daughter's word: "princess." She is beautiful and strong, but we were butting heads. I started seeing her as opinionated and headstrong and we would argue more than we would communicate.

When I turned the frame around, I could see her as the princess she is...that she is a natural leader and has great ideas and strengths that I had missed. Yes, it still takes her an eternity to get ready in the morning, but princesses primp a while...it takes time to look like royalty!

My youngest daughter's word: "precious." She had been struggling with some attitudes that were being picked up from television shows and I began defining her by this new alter ego.

When I heard the word "precious," it reminded me of how God sees her. When I saw her that way and started treating her as precious and speaking that word over her little life, some of that attitude began to melt away.

Of course, cutting out some television shows also helped, but changing my perspective of who she is made an even bigger impact.

God gave me the word "peace" for my husband. Lord, love this man. He has to deal with me on a daily basis!

Our personality types are an interesting mix...mine loves to *party* and his loves *peace*. With my party personality also comes a myriad of emotions which my husband navigates well most of the time.

God knew what I needed in my life!

Unfortunately, sometimes I would not see his peaceful personality as an asset...I began to see my husband through that other side of the frame.

I needed this reminder that God sees my husband as a man of peace and when I see him that way, I can appreciate this gift and know God designed him not to go on emotional roller coaster rides with me!

I felt done with this exercise until God tugged at my heart once more and reminded me that if I didn't see myself the way He sees me, nothing would really change. He dropped the word "perfect" into my heart.

Now I knew that was from God because there is NO way I had ever used that word to describe myself!

All I ever saw were my faults.

There was very little grace I would give myself, but He saw me as perfect. He couldn't love me more than He already did. I have the you-can-do-no-wrong status with Him. He loves me in spite of the mistakes I make.

The more I let this word soak into my spirit, the more I am able to see others through God's eyes.

"I praise you because I am fearfully and wonderfully made; your works are wonderful, I know that full well."
Psalms 139:14 NIV

Reflect & journal:

*Take the time to ask God how He sees your family —
pray that He gives you His perspective for each one.*

*Write them down here and when you interact with
them, whisper the word to yourself and try to even
visualize it like a name tag they wear on their shirt...
or forehead!*

*Don't forget about yourself...what does heaven say
about you?*

. . .

9: Bird-sitting Services

We have a bird couple living in our backyard. Two red cardinals, one is more colorful...we decided she must be the wife!

Although I'm sure there are expert bird watchers who might correct us, we are sticking with it.

As we were packing for a trip overseas, I was stressed about all of the things we needed to do to be sure that we could leave for three weeks. Escaping the chaos for a few minutes, I sat outside and noticed our bird couple swoop down from the trees onto the bird bath.

Instead of just enjoying the peaceful moment,

I started to add them to my list of worries and actually had the crazy thought — do we need a bird sitter?

I knew that didn't make sense. I had never seen commercials or billboards for backyard bird-sitting services.

That being said, I do not pack or prepare for trips in a way that makes sense to a normal person.

I don't just have a simple packing list that I check off...I pick up every item in my home and ask myself the question, "Should I bring this?"

Then, I add it to my checklists. I have so many checklists that I have a master checklist of all my checklists.

I have lists of what I need to buy, what I need to do, what I will need to buy when I get there, last-minute to do lists, last-minute packing lists, a list of all the bags we packed in case we forget what we packed — it's a lot of lists.

I have also developed a fail-proof system so that I will never be without something that I need on a trip at any time.

It goes like this: if I have ever needed something on a trip that I didn't have packed, it goes on the master packing list to be packed for every trip until the end of time.

This practice has led to the forever-packing of an arm sling and a can opener. Things like that.

I even pack an empty bag in case I end up with more stuff than I started with. I basically pack luggage in my luggage.

I also enjoy putting all liquids in separate plastic baggies because there was a leak that one time.

The fact that I started worrying about the possibility of needing bird-sitting services is not sounding as crazy anymore, is it?

It was in that moment that God spoke to my heart that I don't need to live in worry. He will take care of me just like He will take care of these birds.

I don't need to do anything for them. I don't need to pack for them or ask someone to watch them for us or even put out food in little piles for them. God takes care of them...just like in the verse about the sparrows.

"Look at the birds. They don't plant or harvest or store food in barns, for your heavenly Father feeds them. And aren't you far more valuable to him than they are?"
Matthew 6:26 NLT

I needed this reminder not to worry. I deal with worry often. Especially as a mom, I worry about my children and their future. Sometimes I lie awake at night, and I feel the anxiety like it's sitting on my chest.

It is in these moments that I remember that God's Word says that we are not alone.

I sometimes even picture Him holding me like a child...the Bible talks about Him calming our fears and singing songs over us. I envision Him at our bedside singing to us like a mother would sing a lullaby to her child.

"For the Lord your God is living among you. He is a mighty savior. He will take delight in you with gladness. With His love, He will calm all your fears. He will rejoice over you with joyful songs."
Zephaniah 3:17 NLT

Psalms describes how He collects our tears in a bottle. Can you picture Him gently rubbing the tears off of our faces and bottling them?

"You keep track of all my sorrows. You have collected all my tears in your bottle. You have recorded each one in your book."
Psalms 56:8 NLT

He wants you to know today that He is with you and will walk with you through hard times. You don't need to worry.

God cares for you more than the birds, He will take care of you and what you need.

What do you worry about?

Take time now to give it over to God and let the truth sink in that you are not alone. He is always with you and He will provide for all your needs, even the non-bird ones.

Reflect & journal:

I am a visual person..take a minute and draw your best bird as a reminder that God cares for the birds and cares for you so much more — go ahead and make it a bird couple.

. . .

10: Poison Control

We didn't have kids yet, but I had a Poison Control magnet on our refrigerator...this should have served as fair warning to my newlywed husband.

Therefore, it should not have been a surprise when he was awakened from his slumber by his hysterical wife, convinced she had concocted a lethal mixture of cough and cold remedies — and was *dying*.

I promptly told him it was time to call Poison Control and was then shocked to find that my groom was not concerned in the least. In fact, he was irritated that I woke him up for this.

With shaky hands, I managed to speed dial my father who told me to eat some toast to "absorb the poison."

Upon hearing me talking to his new father-in-law, my husband got out of bed, not wanting to look uncaring. He assured my dad that he would, in fact, call Poison Control immediately.

Meanwhile, I flailed into the kitchen to produce the life-saving toast.

I could hear my husband mumbling into the phone, then he walked into the kitchen and said, "Good news...they said you are going to live."

He crawled back into bed. Relieved, I called my father back to cancel the prayer chain.

And then it happened.
I saw it.
Sparks and a FIRE in the toaster oven!

I dropped the phone, ran to get the fire extinguisher screaming, "Fire!" the whole time. My father was still hanging on the line. My husband did not seem phased by the idea of an actual fire, but he did jump up when he heard me cocking the fire extinguisher!

He ran into the kitchen, trying to tackle me before I pulled the trigger.

But it was too late — a thick layer of greenish foam covered the entire room: the toaster, the counters, the floor, the refrigerator...anything I deemed as remotely flammable.

In shock, my husband took the extinguisher from my hands and yelled for me to just go back to bed. He had enough excitement for one night. I heard him pick up the phone and convince my dad of the absence of any fire damage.

Meanwhile, I remembered my toast. In my delirium, I didn't even notice it was green.

Stumbling towards my bedroom, I was eating my green toast. Then, my husband saw me...his eyes widened.

He paused and said, "Dad, I have to go...I need to call Poison Control again."

Poison control — how do we actually control poison? Although we don't usually eat green poison foam, we don't realize that we allow other poisons into our lives.

Negativity can be a poison to our joy. It can kill our hope. Sometimes it seeps in with traces of it here and there during hard times or difficult circumstances until it can poison our whole outlook on life.

The Bible gives us a powerful antidote in Philippians 4:8:

"And now, dear brothers and sisters, one final thing.
Fix your thoughts on what is true, and honorable, and
right, and pure, and lovely, and admirable. Think
about things that are excellent and worthy of praise."
Philippians 4:8 NLT

Think on these things. When we find ourselves drinking the poison of negativity, we need to remember Paul's words to fix our thoughts on things that bring joy.

We should even ask ourselves: is this true? Is it honorable? Is it right and pure? Is it lovely or admirable? What can I think about that would be excellent or worthy of praise right now?

Maybe we need to put 'Poison Control' on speed dial by writing out the Phil 4:8 cure on a sticky note for our refrigerator?

Although...I will still keep the actual Poison Control magnet up there, too, just in case!

Reflect & journal:

Take a few moments to write down some negative thoughts that might be poisoning your outlook on life and stealing your hope. Then, write out the Philippians 4:8 'cure' below them.

. . .

11: Designer Dog

We bought a new puppy this summer. Keyword: *bought.* I did not post any pictures of him on any social media for weeks because I feared the criticism since he was not a rescue...unless you count "rescuing" him from a breeder and paying a hefty *ransom.*

My husband could not believe we would pay money for a dog. "Don't you just find a box of puppies along the road?" he asked as an answer to my begging.

I made my case: he's a "designer dog." Half Maltese and half Yorkie...he's a Morkie.

My husband succumbed, we brought him

home and named him Jax — Jaxson actually.

We paid so much for this designer dog, we should have named him Gucci...or Louie.

A few months later, we took him for his doggie surgery and the vet put an Elizabethan collar around his neck to keep him from his stitches.   It would keep him from hurting himself.

He looked so confused by this "cone of shame" on his head.

What had he done to deserve this? He had a hard time eating or drinking because of this newfound obstacle and watching him try to go up the stairs was almost comical.

He had no idea why this was happening and that it was only temporary.   He thought this cone was his new reality!

He didn't realize it wouldn't be there forever and that this piece of plastic had a purpose and was actually good for him.

The Bible talks about everything working together for good in Romans 8:28,

"And we know that God causes everything to work together for the good of those who love God and are called according to his purpose for them."
Romans 8:28 NLT

There have been times that I have faced an obstacle and I have not seen the good in it. My perspective was definitely woe-is-me, but what is important to remember is that some obstacles are just temporary and they tend to serve a purpose we cannot yet see.

I don't believe God causes the pain we are going through, but He will extract the good out of it and allow it to be used for a purpose in our lives.

He might allow cone-shaped obstacles to be there for a time to safeguard us even if we don't understand why!

This obstacle is not our new reality...it's temporary and we need to trust the One who ransomed us that there is a purpose to our pain and that He will walk through it with us.

"But now, O Jacob, listen to the Lord who created you. O Israel, the one who formed you says, "Do not be afraid, for I have ransomed you. I have called you by name; you are mine. When you go through deep waters, I will be with you. When you go through rivers

67

of difficulty, you will not drown. When you walk through the fire of oppression, you will not be burned up; the flames will not consume you."
Isaiah 43:1,2 NLT

Reflect & journal:

What obstacles have you faced in your life? Take a moment to write down the good that God wants to extract from them. If it helps, write the words, "God will find the good!" across them!

. . .

12: Tin Man

When my sisters and I look back on our childhood family pictures, we notice a common thread...we wore a lot of boyish clothes. We aren't sure if our parents just lacked fashion sense or if they were given a large amount of hand-me-downs from a boys' group home.

We also noticed a trend in that my sisters and I wore a series of child Halloween costumes that were very obviously for boys. One year in particular I remember donning a tin man costume from <u>The Wizard of Oz</u>[3].

This costume literally has the word *man* in its name. I don't remember ever asking to be the tin man. I don't know that anyone in history had ever specifically asked to be this side character, especially without the other characters involved.

I was the lone tin can man...there was no Wizard-of-Oz theme that year. The rest of my family didn't join in as munchkins or a scarecrow. He doesn't even have an actual name.

I'm not sure why Dorothy wasn't the go-to costume. I had long brown hair as a child and I'm pretty sure I owned a dress and a basket somewhere.

I remember standing there on the steps in front of our house in this most uncomfortable silver suit, wearing the plastic mask with the eye holes that made it hard to blink, and the rubber band that pulled my hair while holding it tightly to my face.

We were taking pictures and I could see my friend walking across the street in her cheerleader costume. She was my pretty neighbor friend who all the boys liked.

I remember having the thought even at eight years old as I adjusted the tin cylinder around my waist, "Yep, a cheerleader costume was a better way to go."

To be honest, I don't know how my mom got me to put this hunk of metal on my body...I can't even get my own kids to wear an itchy sweater.

Bringing it full circle, this past Halloween was the first time we went out trick-or-treating with my kids after a long hiatus.

My costume: Dorothy.

Yes, I was a grown woman in pigtails and gingham. I even got my family to join in as the scarecrow and Glinda.

And I got candy.

I became like a child again and I ate all the candy I got within three days. I don't recommend this, but I do understand it. I earned that candy and it was mine. I only shared the gross candy.

I had never liked Halloween...the gore is so over the top. I could never understand how moms who carry Neosporin® in their purses can suddenly think it's cute to dress their kids up with fake blood-soaked shirts or a headband that makes it look like a dagger is somehow lodged in their heads.

I stayed away from the trick-or-treating scene for partly the gore reason and partly because I grew up in a home where after our family found Jesus, we hid in the basement every October 31st like there was an annual zombie apocalypse.

That's what we did back then — your family would either hide out in a type of Halloween protest or leave Jesus tracts on your porch instead of candy.

I recently heard a pastor say that Halloween is the only holiday that our neighbors might open their home (or at least their porch) to the community. It can be an incredible time to reach out, meet our neighbors, and share God's love with them.

Jesus wasn't afraid to engage with the culture. He intentionally hung out with tax collectors and prostitutes to show His love. He made the most of His time on the earth and reached out to people in all walks of life.

I'm not suggesting that our neighbors are tax collectors and prostitutes...although some costumes might give that impression!

I'm saying that God isn't afraid of rubbing up against humanity with all our faults and flaws.

He called a tax collector to be one of His disciples.

He struck up a conversation with the woman at the well whose past could have been a soap opera.

He allowed a forgiven prostitute to wash his feet with her hair.

He touched and healed lepers who had to shout that they were "unclean" wherever they went.

Humanity didn't scare Him.

"As Jesus went on from there, He saw a man named Matthew sitting at the tax collector's booth.
"Follow me," He told him, and Matthew got up and followed Him.
While Jesus was having dinner at Matthew's house, many tax collectors and sinners came and ate with Him and His disciples.
When the Pharisees saw this, they asked His disciples, "Why does your teacher eat with tax collectors and sinners?"

On hearing this, Jesus said, "It is not the healthy who need a doctor, but the sick.
But go and learn what this means: 'I desire mercy, not sacrifice.' For I have not come to call the righteous, but sinners."
Matthew 9:9-13 NIV

Reflect & journal:

Whatever the setting, be willing to share God's love with those around you.   Make a list of a few things you could you do today to reach out to your neighbors.

If you happen to get a bucket full of candy in the process, so be it.

. . .

13: Happy Camper

Growing up, we didn't camp. The phrase "roughing it" on vacation meant our family went to a hotel without a jacuzzi.

When questioned, my dad once told me he did all the camping he ever wanted to do in the army.

My husband, Bryan, hadn't camped much growing up either and so he decided one day that our little family needed to start a new camping era for generations to come.

Our son was seven, our daughter was four, and I was pregnant with our third child when we set out on our expedition. My husband assured me that he would get all the equipment ready and would secure a location near some restrooms.

I wish it was also close to some *restaurants* because I was in charge of bringing the food.

I had no idea what you should pack and eat while camping.   I don't know why I thought we could only eat food out of cans as if we were settlers traveling the Oregon Trail.   Did they have canned foods back then?   I don't know.

SpaghettiOs®, canned raviolis, stew-in-a-can...none of these were appetizing (especially when served at room temperature) and eating like that felt like we were escaping some kind of natural disaster and broke into our emergency prepper stash.

My husband felt proud to be outdoors with his family and the park ranger even visited our campsite.   Bryan, wanting to engage in camp-like conversation with his newfound celebrity, asked him what poison ivy looked like.

That's when the ranger pointed to several areas in and around our campsite and did a large, sweeping motion over the area our children were currently rolling.

He said something to the effect of, "You're going to want to hose them down...and anything that they have touched."

I heard it like he was talking in slow motion.

By the time we finished scrubbing everyone and everything, it was nightfall. This is when we found out that the temperature dropped twenty-five degrees at night and this is when we also found out that our sleeping bags were not rated for outdoor use.

We had a Spider-Man® sleeping bag and a Cinderella® sleeping bag for the kids which were definitely intended for warm sleepovers at friends' houses rather than the northern Californian mountains — i.e., the tundra.

We didn't realize that the inflatable mattress/ raft my husband brought so that his pregnant wife wouldn't sleep on rocks had a hole in it.

I distinctly remember a moment in the middle of that night when I lied there shivering on the deflated plastic and caught Bryan's eye. I mouthed the words: "never again."

By morning, I had convinced him that our multi-day excursion was now just a one-night event and that we would be packing up our things. The park ranger was not surprised.

We were relieved that the kids displayed no signs of getting poison ivy, but my husband's face looked a bit distorted.

By later that day, the swelling increased and formed a type of unicorn horn on Bryan's forehead.

Although we were grateful his unicorn horn wasn't a permanent fixture on his forehead, I wouldn't use the phrase, "happy campers" to describe our weekend experience!

Feeling happy is contingent on our surroundings and our circumstances. Having true joy has little to do with those elements.

Sometimes it's hard for us to remember there's a difference. We think that when the *feeling* of happiness is gone, we don't have joy.

It's possible for us to focus so intently on our circumstances that we miss the big picture of joy all around us.

My husband and I had attended a marriage conference over ten years ago and still remember the speaker holding up a quarter in the sunlight. He talked about how if you hold the quarter close enough to your eye, it can block out the sun.

We remember the quarter illustration every time we allow the circumstances around us to become big enough that they block out true joy in our lives.

Usually, the issues aren't actually very big, but the more we let them overshadow our focus, the larger they become in our eyes.

"Always be joyful. Never stop praying. Be thankful in all circumstances, for this is God's will for you who belong to Christ Jesus."
1 Thessalonians 5:16-18 NLT

Reflect & journal:

Is there a quarter in the way of your joy? What is stopping you from being a happy camper? Hopefully, it's not a poison ivy unicorn horn.

Take a moment to write down these circumstances and reflect on how you can remove them from your focus so you can see the joy around you.
. . .

14: Baking Exchange

Have you ever heard of a Christmas baking exchange? Well, I hadn't. And I'm pretty sure it was the last one our family did since this fateful one...unless they are doing them secretly and I just haven't been invited, which is a definite possibility.

One of my husband's relatives had suggested that in lieu of gifts one year, we would all mail each family a tin of holiday treats. You read that correctly — emphasis on *each* family (i.e., all the families...like 10-15 of them).

I was newly married into this very Southern family with some of the best bakers this side of the Mississippi...well, either side really.

I knew I needed to up my baking game and that my boxed Little Debbies® probably were not quite what they had in mind.

I hurled myself into a whirlwind recipe search for the most impressive of holiday fare.

Fudge!

It's a classic...and I was convinced it had to be my ticket into the Family Dessert Hall of Fame!

I bought all the ingredients; I followed the recipe.

I didn't, however, notice that the recipe called for cream cheese and that it was also a no bake recipe. How would I send this chocolate flavored cream cheese that I made *unrefrigerated* through the *mail?*

It was a bust. I went back to the drawing board, empty tins beckoning me from the counter.

Five days left until send off. I still had time.

I found a recipe for some honey-glazed nuts. There are lots of nuts in Christmas songs...chestnuts and all. I didn't consider the crazy cost of filling multiple tins with nuts; instead, I justified the investment.

I bought the ingredients; I followed the recipe.

But...I read things out of sequence.

I read the recipe like this: take pan of honey-glazed nuts out of oven, let cool, break into pieces.

Instead, I should have read it like this: take pan of honey-glazed nuts out of oven, get nuts off pan immediately before they harden to the pan like mortar and necessitate hours of chiseling and eventual emotional breakdown and throwing said pans into the garbage.

You get the idea.

Two days left until send off. I'm running out of time.

How about a family secret? I enlisted my aunt's help in sending me her time-tested gingerbread boy recipe.

I bought the ingredients; I followed the recipe.

I had to quadruple this recipe and the mound of spices and flour and molasses created a high dome atop my largest bowl.

As I stood in my kitchen trying to figure out how to stir it, my husband came in to heat up his coffee in the microwave.

He grabbed the mug in one swift motion and I watched in horror as the mug hit the top of the microwave, slipped out of his hand, and poured itself directly into my bowl of gingerbread bliss.

It would have been impossible to recreate that mishap if we had tried.

Some say I could have made coffee flavored gingerbread boys, but they weren't physically present to tell me that, now were they?

I sat down on the kitchen floor and laughed so hard. It was a kind of cry-or-laugh choice moment and I chose the latter.

Then, in my delirium, I asked myself, "What do I have a lot of?"

There were no more days. Today was send-off day.

My answer: popcorn...microwave popcorn.

I had no choice and no pride left. I really did it. I sent all the families a batch of microwave popcorn — in a metal holiday tin.

It probably would have been better and less stale if I had sent them an unopened microwave packet of unpopped kernels!

I wasn't surprised when I never received accolades or a request for my popcorn recipe. I did, however, enjoy receiving tins of actual holiday treats.

Sometimes you might feel like you've done it all right...you've bought the ingredients; you've followed the recipe, but life is still not turning out like you expected.

One of my favorite verses in Scripture is one found on many-a plaque, mug, and bumper sticker:

"For I know the plans I have for you," says the Lord.
"They are plans for good and not for disaster, to give
you a future and a hope.
Jeremiah 29:11

But sometimes I like to see the context and look in front of the verse and behind the verse to see what is really going on.

Right before this often-quoted verse, is part of the setting of the story...

"This is what the Lord says: "You will be in Babylon for seventy years. But then I will come and do for you all the good things I have promised, and I will bring you home again."
Jeremiah 29:10 NLT

The Israelites were exiled to Babylon. They had been deported from Jerusalem. Not quite the outcome they were expecting as members of "God's people."

They had bought the ingredients; they had followed the recipe. But things did not look like they were working out.

Some prophets were giving them false hope and proclaiming their quick victory, but Jeremiah had heard from God; it's gonna be a while.

Seventy years, in fact.

God has a plan. It might not look quite like the recipe.

But He makes us promises...promises of hope and a future, of good things and not disaster.

He promises that He will listen when we pray and that if we look for Him wholeheartedly, we will find Him. Promises that He will end our captivity and restore fortunes and bring us home.

Now that sounds like an exchange I wouldn't mind being a part of.

"In those days when you pray, I will listen. If you look for me wholeheartedly, you will find me. I will be found by you," says the Lord. "I will end your captivity and restore your fortunes. I will gather you out of the nations where I sent you and will bring you home again to your own land."
Jeremiah 29:12-14 NLT

Reflect & journal.

Have there been areas of your life where things didn't go as planned? Take a few minutes to write them down and then write next to them: "God has a promise of hope!"

. . .

15: Whack-a-Mole

I have a love-hate relationship with carnivals. I love the fun, electric atmosphere, the booths where the local Boy Scout® troop would sell birch beer, where the church groups peddled their pies, and where crowds gathered at the big, bingo pavilion.

The stage with a local band supplied music as a backdrop to the mayhem of bright lights and varied screams as rides took turns spinning kids and teens into a frenzy.

My issue: the games.

They beckon to my husband: play me, win me, don't worry about how much it costs —

you need that room-sized stuffed animal monkey.

I just can't.

I can't see spending all that money to maybe win something I don't even want. I often wonder where all these creatures go...do people have storage units full of these mammoth things?

I must interject a bit of a confession.

I somehow own two 5'3" stuffed animal bears that my husband did not initiate the adoption of in the slightest. Each of my two daughters begged for one for Christmas and I can't resist a good Christmas moment...with the bear and the bow on top. You get the picture.

I had to smuggle them into our home and I actually thought that I could fit one of them into a trash bag. The trash bag only covered his bear head; and as I tried to run him inside, it looked like I was taking him hostage!

Back to carnival games.

Whack-a-mole is the only game that tempts

me.   There is something strangely satisfying about hitting those moles...being faster, anticipating their next moves.   Maybe I had some angst I was working out, who knows?

Anxious thoughts can sort of pop up like that. Worry seems to pop up in places we don't expect.   If we don't stop these thoughts quickly, they can overwhelm us and steal our joy.

One morning, I was struggling with thoughts of some stressful situations as if they were just waiting for me to crack open my eyes.   They were popping up...one fretful thought after another.   I felt a sense of dread before I even got out of the sleeping position.

In that moment, God reminded me of my carnival days and I pictured myself standing in front of these anxious moles.   I began whacking them as soon as they popped up, not giving them the chance to linger or take root in my heart.

It was the visual I needed to whip the worry, to fight my fears, and to stop the cycle of stress and anxiety.

It sounds simple and even silly, but I can't tell

you how instrumental this mental picture has been to help me see that these anxious thoughts just do not have a place in my day.

We will obviously have to face obstacles and can't run from them, but we don't need the worry to be part of the routine. It has served as an exercise in taking my thoughts captive.

Worry and fear will always be options. We could choose to embrace them at every turn. We could live from one mole to the next, just focusing on the stress of it all.

But God isn't stressed out. He doesn't look at the world's issues and bite His nails or get a knot in His stomach. He doesn't fret or fear. He doesn't even feel the weight of it all.

Do you know how we can know that?

...Because Jesus took naps in the middle of storms.

...Because God sets up a dinner table in the middle of our enemies.

...Because He numbered the hairs on our heads in the middle of the chaos around us.

It has to do with *trust*. We can truly trust that God is able to provide for our every need, give us wisdom in every circumstance, and carry us through every tough time we might face.

I think He's got us covered — and any situation that might pop up.

Don't let the anxiety moles in your life linger: whack them, take your thoughts captive, and then trust in God!

And, who knows? Maybe one day you, too, could even win your very own life-sized stuffed bear hostage.

"Suddenly, a fierce storm struck the lake, with waves breaking into the boat. But Jesus was sleeping."
Matthew 8:24 NLT

"You prepare a feast for me in the presence of my enemies."
Psalms 23:5a NLT

"And the very hairs on your head are all numbered."
Matthew 10:30 NLT

Reflect & journal:

What anxious moles try popping up in your life?
Take a moment to write them down and whack them
by crossing them out and writing the word, "TRUST"
over them!
. . .

16: Couch to Triathlon

I wasn't a runner. It's as if I heard the lifeguard's no-running whistle at a public pool that one time and then just applied it to my whole life.

I was once asked by my doctor if I was active; and I proceeded to tell him how much my husband runs as if that counted by osmosis.

I just don't like it. My body didn't seem built for it. My body was built for lunches and naps and comfy snuggling.

Then, one night my husband and I were watching a TV channel that only had shows about triathlons.

Our TV had about four channels in our language at the time and the other three must have been on a commercial break for me to watch the triathlon channel.

We watched these incredible people with disabilities finishing these races complete with swimming, biking, and running portions. It was inspiring, but even in that moment I said out loud, "I could never do that."

As the words fell from my lips, something didn't feel right. Why did I just discount myself like that? I had four working limbs and everything.

I realized we also had moved onto a college campus where my husband worked and we had access to an indoor olympic-sized pool and a track outside our front door.

I began researching triathlons in my area...mostly to try to find the shortest one possible while still getting credit for doing one.

I learned that there are "sprint triathlons" which sounds like it means fast, but it's more because it's about half of an olympic triathlon. I found one in my area about three months out and signed up. I paid the fee and posted it on social media. Now I had to do it.

Thus began what I called: my "couch-to-triathlon" triathlon.

I trained for three months over a summer, grateful that a new friend offered some free swim coaching lessons and to be my pool buddy several early mornings every week.

You think you know how to swim until you swim across an olympic-sized pool. The pool was always frigid, but by the time I swam back and forth a few times, I was grateful for it since I didn't know you could sweat while swimming.

The running was not my favorite. It was a record hot, Texas summer and even at 5 a.m., it would sometimes hit one hundred degrees.

I started by just walking one mile. Then, I added some running time until I could run the whole first mile. I would then add another walking mile to it and start the process again until I was running five miles every weekday.

I had to borrow a bike. It was an expensive bike, but it was a broken bike. I didn't realize

I needed all the gears to work. I still trained on it, got chased by dogs on it, and flew off of it.

My husband thought I was a beast for riding it home bleeding from the fall, but I didn't have another ride home.

The day of the triathlon was upon me. I got into the lake with my number written on my leg. I looked around and thought, "I should go up to the front of the pack...why isn't everyone wanting to be up front?"

So, I waded through the water and made my way up to the front, then looked around and saw the elite swimmers and had a second thought: "I am going to get killed up here."

I started pushing my way back to the back and my husband, trying to videotape, was confused and thought maybe I was already quitting.

I didn't quit, but I did abandon everything my swim coach friend taught me. When the gun fired and the lake became a blender of flailing arms and kicking legs, all the proper form went out the window as I decided it was best to keep my head above the water and just doggie paddle the whole way.

My husband waited by the lake exit to capture my expression coming up out of the water. He expected a look of exhaustion and possibly regret, but my face had lit up because I had *survived* and I was done with the hardest, possibly life-threatening part.

The biking was next...seventeen miles. I don't think I trained enough. At least not long enough to notice that shifting gears is important.

Or long enough to learn how to hold a cup of water in one hand while still staying upright on the bike.

Or long enough to pass someone...not even old people.

My goal the whole time was just to finish the race before the staff needed to clean it up, but things changed when I saw the motorcycle cop following closely behind the poor last cyclist! I suddenly decided that I could not be that *last* person.

I actually had a desire to quit halfway through the biking portion until I remembered that it was a loop and I was at the other side of it. I would have to bike just as long to quit than to stay in the race!

My legs were made of jello when I got off the bike to run the final part of the race: the 5k.

I had run more than this three miles every day, but not on jello legs. I had planned to run it, but it was looking more appealing to walk it at that point. I knew if I started it by walking, I would never start to run.

So, I pushed past the jello and started running or at least my version of running which is sometimes slower than others can speed-walk.

I made up some of my lost time on the bike ride and managed to pass several people. I think it helped that I had trained outside in the heat rather than on a treadmill in an air-conditioned gym because it was in the high 90s that morning!

Crossing the finish line felt amazing. Not sure which was better: the fact that I had done what I set out to do or the fact that I could stop moving my body now.

My husband and I had stayed around for the trophies just so I could catch my breath.

To my surprise, I got 2nd place in my gender/age category! I told my family and friends. My sister asked how many people were in my category.

I looked it up. Three.

There's a lot of race references in the Bible. God must like running. Not sure I like that He likes running.

One of my favorite passages in the running category is Hebrews 12:1-2:

"Therefore, since we are surrounded by such a huge crowd of witnesses to the life of faith, let us strip off every weight that slows us down, especially the sin that so easily trips us up. And let us run with endurance the race God has set before us. We do this by keeping our eyes on Jesus, the champion who initiates and perfects our faith. Because of the joy awaiting Him, He endured the cross, disregarding its shame. Now He is seated in the place of honor beside God's throne."
Hebrews 12:1-2 NLT

I like the mental picture of a group of Bible heroes cheering us on from the clouds, like there's some bleachers set up and maybe an angelic band or something.

The next verse says that we should strip off the weight of sin that will trip us up so we can be free to run the race God set before us.

It says we can run our race with endurance when we focus on Jesus who is already a champion...His race, His endurance, included carrying the weight of the cross.

He carried that weight so we didn't have to carry ours. We could be free to run because He already carried the weight of sin across the finish line.

I love the way the passage includes what was on Jesus' mind while he was running His race…the joy awaiting Him.

We were His joy. He was thinking about us. And that joy was so strong that it even dispelled the shame of the cross.

You don't have to have run a race or even have watched the triathlon channel on your TV to have won the true prize of knowing God's perfect love for you!

Reflect & journal:

What weight is holding you back from running your race? Take a few moments to write down any issues that are entangling you. Then, hand them over to God to carry so that you can run freely! Draw a picture of a finish line and you crossing it!

. . .

17: Puppets, Towel Cakes, & Silversmithing

I was in a puppet-making club in college...because I liked to party. Yes, it was a real club and I spent hours with the other puppet-making members learning the craft and important things like: how to choose the perfect puppet tongue shape or what size baby clothes to buy for your puppet.

And, maybe most importantly, that I was not quite ready for a high-temp hot glue gun.

After my crazy college days, my husband and I worked as youth and children's ministers in Boston. When our finances didn't quite add up, I decided that I would start a business; yes, a puppet-making and puppet-selling business.

I would be the master creator and exporter of said puppets.

I was convinced this would be a huge hit...it's surprising that more people were not clamoring to be in the puppet business. Besides, I already had all those puppet-producing skills.

I had the cardboard patterns.
I bought the supplies.
It didn't work out.

Apparently, people need to want to buy puppets.

Next, my aunt gave my sister a wedding shower gift — a cake made out of towels. This was my next big break. I begged my sister to let me take it apart so I could reverse engineer it, taking detailed notes and measurements.

I had the prototype.
I bought the supplies.
It didn't work out.

Apparently, I would need to be able to re-create the towel cake at least one time.

Next, I saw a necklace I liked with the names of children stamped into the metal. This was it: I would be a silversmith.

I googled the instructions.
I bought the supplies.
(So much silver I bought.)
It didn't work out.

Apparently, there is a skill set involved in silversmithing...one where you need to be able to stamp the letters next to each other.

Also, maybe most silversmiths don't decide that it's a good time to start the smithing right after having a baby and that maybe banging on metal every nap time isn't the best idea.

So...maybe puppets had their day, maybe it wasn't the season for towel cakes or silver smithing, but I think God delights in us trying new things and exploring the gifts He has given us (or realizing the ones He hasn't).

So many people are paralyzed by perfection...they don't want to try new things because they don't want to do something that God didn't tell them to do directly or because they fear failure. God has blessed us all with special gifts and talents and abilities. I believe

He truly wants us to try them on for size.

Maybe your best contribution to the world is doing that special thing that God made you to love to do.

Granted, I don't think puppets was my thing or cakes made from towels, and I don't feel like I was a born silversmith, but I think God smiled at my efforts in trying something creative and playing with my gifts.

And, I think He knew that, ultimately, I would enjoy telling these crazy stories to groups around the country as part of my comedy sets!

He is a giver of good gifts. He knows the desires of our hearts. He will direct your path...even if it has nothing to do with exporting puppets dressed in baby clothes.

"Whatever is good and perfect is a gift coming down to us from God our Father, who created all the lights in the heavens. He never changes or casts a shifting shadow. He chose to give birth to us by giving us His true word. And we, out of all creation, became His prized possession."
James 1:17-18 NLT

"O Lord, you have examined my heart and know everything about me. You know when I sit down or stand up. You know my thoughts even when I'm far away. You see me when I travel and when I rest at home. You know everything I do. You know what I am going to say even before I say it, Lord. You go before me and follow me. You place your hand of blessing on my head. Such knowledge is too wonderful for me, too great for me to understand!"

Psalms 139:1-6 NLT

Reflect & journal:

What special gifts did God give you that you should be playing with right now? Take a moment to write them down here!

. . .

18: Santa is Dead

Our son was inquisitive...and persistent. He asked a lot of questions. Sometimes this meant he got the answers he wanted in the form of an exasperated sigh and shocking phrases blurted out without much discretion.

By the time our second grader finished interrogating us, he drilled down to what he wanted: the truth. Santa was dead.

We envisioned years more of cookies positioned by the fireplace, but we did not picture the reality that our son would be a crusader for justice and lone star of veracity.

He dug deep until we broke and confessed that Saint Nick had died years ago, but that his legend lived on in the hearts and minds of children. Satisfied with his newfound wisdom, he moved on to other conquests involving cardboard construction; his curiosity quenched.

Then, it happened.

The next day as I walked closer to the classroom to pick up our son from school, I watched some of his young classmates filter out with red, wet faces and snorts and sniffles. Parents escorting them in a sort of hug-walk.

What was going on? I hurried in.

Our son looked fine, backpack strapped on and ready to go. His teacher did not look fine. She glared a bit in my direction.

She pushed a piece of paper into my hands and said, "Thanks...and yes, it was your son."

Confused, I looked down at the words on the letter addressed to every parent in her class. I caught the words "Santa" and "dead" and, suddenly, all became clear.

Years later, Christmas is still my favorite holiday...even in the absence of Santa.

I kind of like getting credit for the gifts I painstakingly research, bargain-hunt, procure, hide, wrap, and tag!

While looking over my Christmas list one year, I overheard my son talking to his friend on the phone and his words made me cringe.

He told his friend that he had wanted something for Christmas but that it was too expensive. Then he said, "Yeah, my parents might spend like $100 on me and that's if — I've been REALLY good."

Hearing my son say those words, "If I've been REALLY good" almost hurt my heart. Is that what he really believes? Does he think we are tallying up his failures and triumphs to come up with his net worth?

I didn't realize that he thought how many gifts we gave him for Christmas depended on his behavior.

We never based his Christmas presents on that. We have always given him gifts because he is our son.

I love how God uses these moments in our lives to illustrate the things He wants to teach us.

God is not keeping track of our mistakes and shortcomings and weighing them against our good moments on some kind of cosmic scale to determine the amount of love He will give to us!

Some of us might even picture God having long *naughty* and *nice* lists, but when we have a relationship with Him and He is our Father, He took the list of naughty things we have done and cast it as far as the East is from the West!

"For His unfailing love toward those who fear Him is as great as the height of the heavens above the earth. He has removed our sins as far from us as the East is from the West."
Psalms 103:11-12 NLT

Know His love for you has no end and has nothing to do with the amount of good you have done or how much you have done wrong in your lifetime — even if you told a whole class of 2nd graders that Santa Claus was dead.

*"But God showed his great love for us by sending
Christ to die for us while we were still sinners."
Romans 5:8 NLT*

Reflect & journal:

Have you ever thought God's love for you was measured out based on your behavior? Rest knowing that He loves you in the middle of your shortcomings. Write a love note to your Heavenly Father for His unconditional love for you!

. . .

19: Three Hour Tour

I don't have a realistic view of time. I don't know why my husband still trusts me when I say I will only be five minutes... especially in any type of building that sells things.

This trait, however, carries over into any type of time-related activity.

While on a cross-country road trip, we had decided to take the kids to Washington, D.C. to see as much of the city as humanly possible. We were headed up the coast to meet some friends, but had budgeted time to be in the city...a whole three hours.

If you have ever been to Washington, D.C., you know parking your vehicle could take three hours.

Instead of paring down our planned itinerary complete with museum stops, all the major monuments and key landmarks, I convinced my husband we could do it all — just faster.

We managed to find a parking spot that was limited to three hours: perfect. After the three-hour mark it became a tow-away loading zone, but we will be back by then anyway, right?

With a preschooler and stroller in tow, we raced away from our van like we just entered a competition.

Crazily running past historical monuments, we would point and shout information to our confused children who had been roused from slumber for this deranged tour of our capital city.

The highlight (and the only thing that our son seemed interested in doing) was seeing the president's house. I think that our son thought the president would be outside mowing the lawn so that he could talk to him about domestic affairs...like the toys he wanted to receive during his time in office.

So, we made sure taking pictures in front of the White House was on our list.

Check.

We even managed to step foot in one of the Smithsonian museums just to say we took our children there...and it was free.

Check.

We didn't let them look around because it was time — we had fifteen minutes to get back to our van before it would be towed!

We started running in the direction of our van in a state of panic, the stroller hitting speeds those plastic tires were never meant to experience. Realizing we would never make it in time as a family unit, I opted to keep the kids while my husband ran ahead to avert the tow truck.

I caught my breath and somehow managed to buy some postcards along the way. When we met up with my husband, I found out that we had already gotten a hefty parking ticket, but we were grateful that he beat the tow truck.

I guess the museum wasn't so free after all!

We were back on the road and were probably a good thirty minutes outside the city when I pulled out the postcards that I had purchased.

I was looking at them and had the thought that these postcards made the White House look better than it did in person.

I compared them to the digital pictures I had taken of our family in front of the tour highlight. It was then that I discovered that we had taken our pictures at the *back* of the White House.

We had never shown the kids the front of the building. In our haste, we had missed the one thing that had mattered most!

Sometimes in our harried schedules, we miss the most important thing. We settle for quick glimpses of what looks like the real deal only to find we never truly engaged.

It's easy to skim through times of reading the Word or get caught up in the activities that fill our calendars and miss knowing who God is and what He might be trying to speak to our hearts in the middle of the chaos.

Slow down.
Breathe deep.

> *"I want you woven into a tapestry of love, in touch with everything there is to know of God. Then you will have minds confident and at rest, focused on Christ, God's great mystery. All the richest treasures of wisdom and knowledge are embedded in that mystery and nowhere else. And we've been shown the mystery! I'm telling you this because I don't want anyone leading you off on some wild-goose chase, after other so-called mysteries, or 'the Secret.'"*
> *Colossians 2:2-4 MSG*

Even though Paul was talking more about the believers not being distracted by other teachings, I think we can be distracted by our own "wild-goose chases" in life these days!

I definitely have found myself on a few.

Instead, try to slow down and drink in the real treasure of who God is and ask Him what He wants to say to your heart today.

Lesson learned — an expensive one at that.

Not that I won't ever underestimate time

again, but I will try not to miss the real, most important things because of a wild goose chase through life...or any other capital cities.

Reflect & journal:

What wild-goose chases have been distracting you or keeping you from being at rest? Take a few moments to list them out and give them over to God. Slow down and breathe in God's deep love for you!

. . .

20: Chicken Salad for the Soul

I was introduced to real chicken salad at my mother-in-law's Southern kitchen table. There were no cans involved in the making of this chicken salad.

It had actual cooked chicken and spices and grapes and slivered almonds involved. I did not know chicken salad was allowed to have more than two ingredients.

My husband and I worked with inner city youth in Boston at the time and our residence was inside the actual church building.

Before you start envisioning us sleeping on pews, I must say that we had a bed and a small kitchen and a bathroom with a toothbrush holder and everything. The apartment was built by volunteers for the would-be staff.

Money was extremely tight and I made a part-time job of coupon clipping. I wish I was one of those people who could finish at the checkout with their coupons and somehow the store owed *them* money!

It was not quite like that.

I decided that week that I would love to make that *wonder* chicken salad recipe. I wrote out the ingredients on my grocery list and tallied up the anticipated total.

It was too high. I sadly whispered something like, "I guess missionaries don't get fancy chicken salad" as I erased the ingredients from the list.

After my shopping trip, we were going over to our pastor's house. His wife walked in the door late as she was coming in from a speaking event and she was holding a huge bowl that she almost couldn't carry herself.

She managed to get the vat onto the counter with some huffing involved.

Her words: "Dorie, do you happen to want this chicken salad? The event had so much left over, they sent me home with it."

I just stood there, dumbfounded and teary-eyed.

I had never seen so much fancy chicken salad in one place; and it had the cooked chicken, the spices, the grapes, the nuts...it was right there as if God had followed my recipe.

I had not told my pastor's wife about my shopping trip earlier that day and how we couldn't afford the ingredients for chicken salad. God wanted to show up for me in such a personal way...answering a prayer I never even officially prayed.

His timing is perfect. It is not as if I am routinely offered big bowls of chicken salad. In fact, I had never before or even in the twenty years since been offered a vat of chicken salad.

The best part: I didn't even have to make it!

God knows the desires of our hearts even before we think or speak them. I picture Him getting a bit giddy as my pastor's wife loaded that vat of chicken salad into her car that night!

I love the Scripture found in Ephesians 3:16-20:

"I pray that from his glorious, unlimited resources He will empower you with inner strength through His Spirit. Then Christ will make His home in your hearts as you trust in Him. Your roots will grow down into God's love and keep you strong. And may you have the power to understand, as all God's people should, how wide, how long, how high, and how deep His love is. May you experience the love of Christ, though it is too great to understand fully. Then you will be made complete with all the fullness of life and power that comes from God. Now all glory to God, who is able, through His mighty power at work within us, to accomplish infinitely more than we might ask or think."
Ephesians 3:16-20 NLT

May you know how deep and wide God's love is for you that your roots might be buried deep in it!

He is ready to do more in and through us than we have even asked or thought...even something as small as providing a vat of fancy, Southern-style chicken salad!

Reflect & journal:

Do you have a chicken salad story of your own? Look for ways God is showing His love for you even before you ask or imagine them.

. . .

21: Mute Hunchback

So, I might have bragged a bit to my kids that I was a theater star in high school. I thought I remembered my days in the spotlight accurately.

However, I recently took my daughters to see a musical at a large community theater and found out the sad truth.

As I sat in the darkness recounting my old theater glory days in quiet whispers, I realized that this rendition of the musical was exactly the same as the one our high school theater performed with only one exception: my character performed a solo that I know I never sang.

My theater director must have made only one

change to the script and cut the only song my character had sung in the score!

It was also in that moment that it came to my remembrance that I had previously played other characters with no vocal cords necessary at all.

Besides the occasional part as scenery in elementary school, during my freshman year of high school, I was given the role of a hunchback.

A male, mute hunchback.

This wouldn't be a bad thing if the musical was based on the *Hunchback of Notre Dame*.[4]
It wasn't.

The directors made sure to emphasize that I was mute and also that I should just sway in the background instead of singing or dancing with the rest of the ensemble.

This character wasn't even in the script — he was written in specifically for me.

The show was set in the days of Christopher Columbus and all my friends' costumes were ornate, layered dresses with petticoats underneath, large lacy bonnets and matching jewels.

My costume consisted of an assortment of ripped rags, a gray wig (oh, because he was also old), and a patch that one of the crew made to look like a droopy eye that I got to glue on my face for every show.

I'm guessing I blocked these roles out of my memory banks whenever I reminisced about my days as a teen Broadway hopeful!

"There are no small parts," they say, "just small actors."

Although I think that was something our moms told us when we were cast as a tree or a cloud, it's not true at all in real life.

We all have small parts in the bigger story...the bigger God-sized story going on all around us. We aren't the main character in this cosmic play.

King David acknowledges his relatively small part this way,

"When I consider your heavens, the work of your fingers, the moon and the stars, which you have set in

place, what is mankind that you are mindful of them,
human beings that you care for them?"
Psalms 8:3-4 NIV

The climax of the book of Job is a powerful
scene that also highlights this contrast. After
being criticized by friends and discouraged by
his wife, Job began to question God's ways.

God answered his "Why me?" questions from
a whirlwind:

"Where were you when I laid the foundations of the
earth? Tell me, if you know so much. Who determined
its dimensions and stretched out the surveying line?
What supports its foundations, and who laid its
cornerstone as the morning stars sang together and all
the angels shouted for joy?"
Job 38:4-7 NLT

Only a few months into our early days in
ministry in Boston, I felt the Lord tell me to
read the book of Job in one sitting.

There were two issues with this: I wasn't a big
reader and I didn't like the story of Job
because I thought it was a bit of a downer.

I finally conceded and read it from start to
finish. I had been going through a season
when I was asking a lot of *why me's*,

questioning God at every turn and I wanted answers.

My husband and I were newlyweds and we had been living in people's spare rooms and our pastor's attic for six months while we waited for volunteers to finish construction of a small apartment inside the church.

We slept on a mattress on the floor and splurged on a name-brand cereal only to have the mice beat us to it.

I started to mope. I started to question our calling. *We didn't even belong in the inner city,* I thought. *Why would you bring us here, God?*

I stood up after reading the last word of the book of Job, feeling unchanged by it.

I started to walk out of the bedroom when I heard almost audibly, "Where were you?"

I had never quite understood the story of Job, but in that moment I knew God was reminding me that He was God and I was not.

He was the creator of the universe and I was not.

I broke down and cried out, "I wasn't there! I wasn't there when You laid the foundations of the earth! I wasn't there!"

It's amazing how God can remind you how small you are but also how important you are in the same moment.

The more we recognize how big God is and how small of a part we play, the more it means when He involves us in His story.

The more it means when He loves us unconditionally.

The more it means that He cares for us and provides for us and gives us peace and joy in our lives.

The more it means that He offers us *hope* and a future.

Reflect & journal:

What can you do today to recognize the bigger God-size story going on all around you and how amazing it is that God wants us to play a part in it?

(Maybe draw a hunchback on the page as a visual... make sure he is mute, though!)
. . .

Hope looks good on you!

Notes

1. Ten Boom, Corrie., John L Sherrill, and Elizabeth Sherrill. *The Hiding Place*. Washington Depot, Conn.: Chosen Books; [distributed by Revell], 1971. Print.

2. Ten Boom, Corrie., *Clippings from my Notebook*. Nashville, Tenn.: Thomas Nelson, Inc., 1982-06-01. Print.

3. Vidor, King, et al. The Wizard of Oz. Metro-Goldwyn-Mayer (MGM), 1939.

4. Hugo, Victor, 1802-1885. *The Hunchback of Notre-Dame*. Notre-Dame De Paris. London : New York : Dutton,Dent; 1973. Print.

About the Author

Dorie Mclemore is a comedian/minister/ story-teller/joy-bringer who believes that caffeine is keeping her alive, popcorn should have its own food group, dry-cleaning saves marriages and that true joy comes from knowing we are worthy of God's love in the middle of all our imperfections.

She has been speaking and performing stand-up comedy since 2006 for audiences coast-to-coast and around the globe. She also travels with comedian Michael Jr., Sisters United, and the carpool line for two different schools.

She is available for speaking engagements, contact information can be found at www.doriecomedy.com

Amish Friendship Bread Recipe, from chapter 3

(Note: this is my official reminder not to publish a cookbook)

Starter ingredients:
1 pkg. active dry yeast
1/4 cup warm water
1 cup flour
1 cup sugar
1 cup warm milk
Wooden spoons *(I guess spoons are ingredients)*
Non-metal bowl *(no idea why it can't be metal)*

Step 1:
How to make the starter:
Soften active dry yeast with 1/4 cup of water for about 10 minutes. Stir with a wooden spoon, not metal. In a non-metal bowl, combine the 1 cup of flour and 1 cup of sugar. Slowly add the 1 cup of warm milk and the dissolved yeast. Cover loosely and let stand. Mixture will become bubbly. This is considered Day 1 of the recipe. *(And all that is only step 1 of 10. This should scare you.)*

Step 2:
On Day 2 for convenience, pour the batter into a gallon plastic bag. Mash the batter in the bag. *(I like how they mention "convenience" in this 10-day recipe)*

Step 3:
Days 3-5 continue to mash the bag once a day. If air pressure fills the bag, let it out.

Step 4:
Day 6 Add 1 cup of flour, 1 cup of sugar, and 1 cup of milk to the bag. Mash the bag.

Step 5:
Days 7-9 mash the bag.

Step 6:
Day 10 Pour the entire contents of the bag into a non-metal bowl — do not use metal spoons. Use wooden or plastic spoons. Add 1.5 cups flour, 1.5 cups sugar, and 1.5 cups milk. *(I'm kind of curious what would happen if we use metal...there are a lot of warnings)*

Step 7:
Measure out 4 separate batters of 1 cup each into one-gallon plastic bags. Date the bags. This is Day 1 of the new starters. Put one bag aside for yourself. Give 3 bags away to friends with a copy of the recipe. They will leave the starter alone for Day 1. You made the starter on the first Day 1, but now the cycle has begun again. Everyone has starter, so Day 1 is the day to leave the starter alone.
(This is where things went awry with my recipe...I just kept dividing the starter!)

Step 8:
To the remaining batter, add the following and mix thoroughly with wooden or plastic spoons:

3 eggs, 1 cup of oil, 1/2 cup milk, 1 cup sugar,

2 tsp cinnamon, 1/2 tsp vanilla extract, 1.5 tsp baking powder, 1/2 tsp. baking soda, 1/2 tsp salt, 2 cups flour, 1 box instant vanilla pudding mix.
(Is it crazy to anyone else that there are still 2 more steps?)

Step 9:
Grease 2 large loaf pans. In a separate bowl, mix 1/2 cup of sugar and 1.5 tsp cinnamon. Dust the greased pans with 1/2 the mixture. Pour the batter evenly into the 2 pans and sprinkle the remaining sugar mixture on top.

Step 10:
Bake 1 hour on 325 degrees or until cooked through. Cool until bread loosens from pan.
(Can you even imagine burning this bread after all this?)

Step 11: *(added by me)*
Enjoy. Although this bread is tasty, maybe just make a cake from a mix next time. You can literally have cake in like 1 hour.

Above: after pic of dollhouse reno, chapter 2
Below: my robber disguise, chapter 4

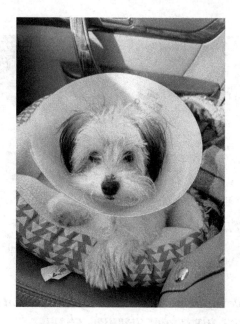

Above: our designer dog in a cone of shame, chap. 11
Below: our happy campers before hosing them down, chapter 13

Above: me, in my creepy tin man costume, chapter 12
Below: me, finally as Dorothy, also chapter 12

Above: the 2 bears I smuggled into our home, chapter 15
Below: me with my 2nd place triathlon trophy (out of 3 people), chapter 16

Above: one of my puppet club puppets I made, chapter 17
Below: the back-of-the-White-House family photo, chapter 19

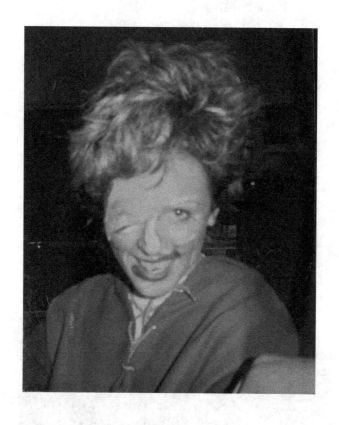

Above: me as the mute hunchback in case you didn't believe me, chapter 21

THIS PAGE INTENTIONALLY LEFT BLANK
I don't know why, but it was intentional.

Acknowledgments

I want to acknowledge and thank, first and foremost, the Lord for inspiring me to write this book, for orchestrating these stories in my life, and for allowing me to articulate them with some of the truth in His Word. I'm thankful for the hope and joy He has brought to my life.

I'm grateful for my husband, Bryan, who has been present for many of these stories and still loves me! He has always encouraged me in anything I have expressed interest in...even the crazy ones! Thank you, Bryan, for your unconditional support and love and for seeing potential in me before I do, even buying me a suitcase when God spoke to you about my traveling to minister.

I'm thankful for my three amazing children, Brendan, Makenna, and Kayley, who have starred in some of these stories and who provide so much light in my life. Thank you for all your encouraging words, for the sticky notes all over my room, for the times you would read my work out loud, and give me what I needed to keep writing. I appreciate and love you more than my heart can handle.

Thank you, mom and dad, for always believing the very best of me from day one of my life. For your unwavering support and continuous investment you make in me every time I venture out in something new. I feel incredibly blessed to have parents with that kind of love for me who cheer me on in everything I do.

I am truly blessed with the best parents-in-law, and three sisters who think I'm a bit crazy but also have been an unbelievable support in my world. Thank you, mom and dad, for loving this Jersey girl and welcoming me in as an honorary Texan and embracing my personality. So thankful for you, Missy and Sandy, for the childhood memories I have had with you — we were truly blessed to grow up that way and for being my best friends as adults, inspiring me as I watch your creativity soar. Thank you, Misty, for your love and acceptance of me when I married your brother and for being such a close confidant, friend, and sister.

My brother-in-laws are pretty awesome. They are the best brothers-I-didn't-know-I-needed! I feel all-around blessed and thankful for the family and extended family God has given me and has brought so much stability in my life.

I also want to acknowledge and thank the incredible friends God has blessed me with in every season of my life and for all time...

The ones who have lived through some of these stories or heard them a million times, the ones who were with me as early as kindergarten and know I kissed a boy during nap time, the ones who were there during awkward middle school haircuts, my youth group friends, my mission trip friends, my college friends, my Boston ministry friends, my Napa and California friends and pizza moms who were my sanity during our baby years, my precious Texas friends, my travel ministry friends, my overseas missionary friends, my comedy friends, my small group friends, my brave beauties, my pink ladies and kiva — love you all and so grateful for every moment God has given me with you.
It's been a lifetime of support.

Definitely feel like I am accepting an Emmy. But they would have played the music and kicked me off the stage by now.

I will write less next time, but this first time I just couldn't help it.

Thank you for everything.

CPSIA information can be obtained
at www.ICGtesting.com
Printed in the USA
LVHW081504120722
723334LV00004B/200

9 781736 219416